The Football Poet

Poetry of a Life's Journey

Darryl Sampson

The Football Poet
Copyright © 2024 by Darryl Sampson

All rights reserved. No part of this publication may be reproduced, distributed, or transmitted in any form or by any means, including photocopying, recording, or other electronic or mechanical methods, without the prior written permission of the author, except in the case of brief quotations embodied in critical reviews and certain other non-commercial uses permitted by copyright law.

Tellwell Talent
www.tellwell.ca

ISBN
978-0-2288-1384-2 (Hardcover)
978-0-2288-1383-5 (Paperback)
978-0-2288-1385-9 (eBook)

Pre-Game Message

This poetry book is about enjoying life, finding satisfaction in the work you do and in whatever you do, and doing it to the best of your abilities. It is about the challenges you experience as you journey through a lifetime, challenges which shape the person you become.

I immigrated to Canada from Trinidad and Tobago when I was eight years old. I was unaware of the hopes and dreams a new country would provide. I found adapting to an unfamiliar environment and culture challenging but informative at an incredibly early age.

I was fortunate to find and have a successful athletic start early in my life at the age of thirteen, winning my first city basketball championship in public school in 1977. Over the next four years I won four consecutive city basketball championships in high school. In my last year of high school, I also won the city football championship.

I was an MVP and All-Star in both basketball and football. I was also an honour roll academic student in high school. I was recruited to play both football and basketball at the university level, but I decided to follow the path of a football career.

After four years at York University, I graduated with two degrees: A bachelor's degree in economics and a bachelor's degree in law and society. I played running back and defensive back for the football team, never winning a championship. Yet, to my amazement, I was drafted the sixteenth pick overall by the Winnipeg Blue Bombers in the 1986 Canadian Football League College Draft.

I played eleven years in the Canadian Football League, retiring after the 1996 season. I participated in four Grey Cup championships, winning in 1988 and 1990. I was a Canadian Football League All-Star in 1993.

After my playing career, I began coaching at York University and then professionally with the Winnipeg Blue Bombers from 2001 to 2003. In 2004, I was inducted into the Winnipeg Blue Bombers Hall of Fame.

When I left the coaching ranks, I began a career in the accounting field where I am currently working for a charitable organization in the Toronto area as a finance and accounting manager.

Becoming a professional Canadian Football League athlete was a daunting and life-impacting experience. It required a dedication and commitment to honing a craft that very few people will fully comprehend.

Poetry, on the other hand, provides that avenue to express the emotion, passion, thoughts, and insights that are the creative embodiment of experiencing and breathing life which anyone can understand.

I am amazed by the insights of the Bible's Book of Ecclesiastes that inspired me to shape this poem titled "Nothing Better."

Nothing Better

This is the day the Lord has made. Be glad and rejoice in it.

By the sweat of your brow, you will eat your food until you return to the ground, since from it you were taken; for dust you are and to dust you will return.

A person can do nothing better than to eat and drink and find satisfaction in their work.

There is nothing better for a person than to be joyful and do good while they live.

There is nothing better for a person than to enjoy their work, because that is their lot.

It is good and proper for a person to eat and drink, and to find satisfaction in their toilsome labour under the sun during the few days of life God has given them—for this is their lot.

It is commended to enjoy life, because nothing is better for a person under the sun than to eat and drink and be glad. Then joy will accompany them in their work all the days of life God has given them under the sun. Go, eat your food with gladness, and drink with a joyful heart, for it is now that God favours what you do. Always be clothed in white, and always anoint your head with oil. Enjoy life with your spouse, who you love, all the days of this meaningless life that God has given you under the sun—all your meaningless days. For this is your lot in life and in your toilsome labour under the sun.

Whatever your hand finds to do, do it with all your might, for in the grave, where you are going, there is neither working nor planning nor knowledge nor wisdom. Be joyous, young one, while you are young, and let your heart give you joy in the days of your youth. Follow the ways of your heart and whatever your eyes see, but know that for all these things God will bring you to judgement. Therefore, fear God and keep his commandments, for this is the whole duty of humanity. God will bring every deed into judgement, including every hidden thing, whether it is good or evil.

I am also influenced by this inspirational poem titled "A Pro" that reminds me to do everything to the best of my capabilities.

A Pro

A pro is a man, not a child.
He is a true craftsman
Who takes pride in his work.
He needs no coddling,
No pep talks, no psychology.
He is paid to produce.
He has enough pride and
Self-respect never to be caught

Giving less than his best.
If you think you are good,
Then why not be better?
If you think you are better,
Then why not be the best?
Title by J.P.

In life you will find that there is always someone who is better than you at something. But there will never be anyone who is the best you. The poem "A Pro" motivates me to always be my best.

This book of poems looks at a life's journey of finding oneself and becoming the best of who you can be.

This book reflects on finding one's beginning, identifying one's purpose, being in love, and finding love. Some poems take an inside look into the deception of the world, its vanities and foolishness.

There are reflections on challenges in life and how we respond to them.

This book also amazes at the beauty, power, and majesty of nature as you journey through life.

Most importantly, throughout this poetic journey, this book takes an inside look at finding God and how he permeates through the life of a person.

The previous two poems were the starting point in inspiring me to depict my journey in life in the poetic form of storytelling.

My goal is to provide a glimpse into a life's journey that also captures a portrait of anyone's journey in this world.

This poetic life story is layered as a game in life, sectioned off in the quarters of a lived experience, with an overtime of insights shared.

I hope that you will find some joy and insight from this life story.

FIRST QUARTER

Finding a Trumpet

Come, play with me, calls
The trumpet,
Louis Armstrong style
Of songs.
Teacher looks at you,
Tall and strong.
Tuba the one for you.
Music pours from your soul
As the owl cry with
Broken leg in tow,
Broken now of heart,
Never to hear the
Sweet note in air.
Tap of fingers lost
Of its rhythms,
Longing to find its true joy.
Something must hold its place,
Finding purpose in this world.
Brown leather bounce on
Pavement cold
Eases the pain of an
Image forlorn.
Now, lyrics strung on courts
Where passion reign of
Dreams unlived
Heralds the tunes of
Sound and dance,
Mi amore.

Atomic Dawg

Big Dawg, Big Dawg,
Big Diggity Dawg.

Dig Dawg, Dig Dawg,
Dig Diggity Dawg.

Sip Dawg, Sip Dawg,
Sip Diggity Dawg.

Hot Dawg, Hot Dawg,
Hot Diggity Dawg.

Where is the Funk?
Who got the Funk?

Atomic Dawg.

My Hero

What are heroes?
Who makes idols?
Why do we look up?
Some are in books.
Some are in the telly.
Some are in the movies.
Others are on the fields.
Only one has captured me.
It is the one who saved me.

Sweetness

In came the doctor with skills astute,
The gale as swift as the deer aloof.
Magic at hand, with spark—a poof.
Air floating on clouds above the roof.
Yes, sweetness was my proof.

Secret Place

Oh! morning I rise.
Oh! evening I sit.
My thoughts perceived afar,
Going out, coming in,
All my ways known
Behind, before hemmed in.
Knowledge lofty to behold.
Presence above and below
On wings of dawn,
The far seaside,
Hand that guides me,
Darkness becoming like light.
My inmost being created,
Woven secretly in place,
Fearfully and wonderfully made
With annals to ordain.
Precious are your thoughts,
Vast among the sand.
Search my open heart.
Test my nervous thoughts.
Throw off what hinders.
Lead me to everlasting.

Strength

I must be strong.
I shall be strong.
God bless those
Who are strong:
Strong in faith,
Strong in righteousness,
Strong in spirit,
Strong in love,
Strong in mind,
Strong in belief,
Strong in Christ
Our Saviour.

A Call

I just called to say
I love you.
I just called to say
I care.
A fire is burning
In my heart.
I just called to say
I miss you,
A burning ever so strong.
I just called to hear
Your voice,
My thoughts, all of you.
I just called to say
    Hello.

Two Lovers

From dusk to dawn,
From life to death,
From being there,
Not being there,
A want, a need,
You can impart.
It's what I feel,
My only one,
For life is love
Which we must do.
Lovers we are too.

Times

Gentle times,
Grim times,
Special times,
Hurtful times,
Caring times,
Painful times,
Sharing times,
Stolen times,
Learning times,
Growing times,
Joy is made for such times.

Bengal Boys

Everybody is talking 'bout
The best team in town.
It's the team from Lester B.
Everybody's jamming down.

All we do is pass the ball,
Drive straight to the hoop,
One hand, two hands, tomahawk,
Reverse, and alley hoop.

Come on, people, fill the stands.
Make a lot of noise.
Clap your hands.
Stomp your feet.
Support the Bengal boys.

The games we play
Are never slow
'Cause we just
Run and gun.
Intense defence is our cheer.
Our man is on the one.

People say we aren't that good
But little do they know
That our team is number one.
Let's, go, go, go.

So, all we need
To pull it through
Is your support
And we'll succeed.

Involvement

The warmth of your touch is what I long.
The fragrance of your soul is ever strong.
The glow of your eyes sparkles as the moonlit sea.
The smile from your lips is the joy I need.
The sweet sound of your voice enlightens my mind.
The soft curves of your body I like to find.
The confines of your heart I love to wander.
The body you possess I desire to enter.
The sensations you give me are truly real
For the presence of you is what I feel.

Luck of Hand

In all the time I waited,
The turmoil increased its measure.
I prayed for a lending grasp
That stemmed a line of hope,
The touch of your hand
The stronghold of my luck,
Fate my chance to escape
From examination.
I was elated with knowledge
That you were a contented part.
I relished intimately
At such thought,
Feeling your presence
Ever demanding.
What more can be expressed?
I'm glad you were there,
Ever so an influence.

Counting the Ways

How do I love thee?
Let me count the ways.
Forbearing all the joys of heart,
It is exhilarating
Beyond compare,
Beyond infinity.
Blessed is our union.
It is fate.
I exist for thee.
Life is no more.
You are mine forever
No one is your match.
Truly, it's divine
In this light
That we may shine.
We were created
"To be as one."

Spiritual Perception

You see but you are blind.
You hear but you are deaf.
You're armed with a weapon
That can build up or destroy,
Sharper than a sword.
Open your eyes and truly see.
Open your ears and truly hear.
All things will be made clear.

Foundation

The root supplies the tree with its strength.
It stems from what is planted.
Sow the good seed that is given from God.
Nourish it with the word of God and his will,
For it will not be upheaved.
It is grounded on solid foundation.

SECOND QUARTER

Echo in the Night

You are the echo of my soul,
The soundboard for the strings
Of my heart,
A majestic note played quietly
At night,
Flowing softly on streams
Downriver,
Waking my restful slumber.

A Heartbeat

I want to always chase you, and conquer you in our love relationship.
I want to have the challenge of seducing the most desirable woman in my life.
I want to wake up, and I long to smell the sweet scent of your hair,
Caress the softness of your skin,
Be in the light of your radiant face.
I want to feel my body tremble from your mere presence,
The whisper of your voice,
The caring stroke of your loving hand.
I want you stored in my heart as treasure,
Locked in a chest, precious and protected, without tarnishing or fading.
I want to be your knight who will honour, respect, and love you until his death beyond.
I want to be all that you want me to be and more.
My love will never subside or die.
I want you to mean more to me than my own life.
I cannot see myself existing without you.

Words Whispered

Remembering the good times of picture frames, collages, and snapshots,
Video images long past,
Scenes of fiery hearts burning,
Passion escalating.
Body tremble, face smile, and the mind
Knows the reason why.
Voice trumpet romance and care.
Please, more to share.

Confronted

We listen but don't hear.
We see but don't observe.
We speak but don't convey.
When we humble ourselves
Then we understand, perceive,
Become aware.

A Match

You light a match,
Unaware of the wind.
Does it blow north, south,
East, or west?
No one can tell.
We wait for a flame,
Not expecting a blaze.
A fire is conceived.
By that time, we are deceived.
Some escape.
Others reach three degrees.
Careful of the fire.
Discretion is not its desire.

The Eyes

We see with the eyes.
See through the eyes with conscience and heart.
Then, we will see beyond the surface of things.

Change

Be prepared for change!
When you least expect it, that's when you will receive it.
Yes, we know that all things change.
Does this change happen when we are ready to change or change it?
Does some other force of change exist?
Why does this change occur?
Why does it change for me?
I am aware of the purpose of change.
It has made me realize my efforts and accomplishments are futile and temporal.
There is no gain in what I have attained.
Why am I challenged by change?
It confuses, bewilders, upheaves, mostly stresses.
What instruction does change have for me?
What lesson must I continually learn?
Change be not a never-ending process.
I must be willing to accept change as part of my maturity.
I must develop perseverance, patience, and faith,
My reliance not on myself but the one who never changes.
Standing firm lest I fall the least among them all,
Eternal trusting one sojourning through time.

Indomitable You

The human spirit,
The human will,
Capable of amazing things
When pushed to breaking,
When nowhere to turn,
And the ultimate action
Is the indomitable one
Where mind, soul, body
Take form greater than mountains,
Moveable by deeds
Unimaginable, supreme
Beyond mortal beings
And galaxies unseen.

Masquerade

Hidden in the construct of the inner being,
Revealed by happenstance,
This-for-that, tit-for-tat.
What do you know?
Bordered by surfaces oblique,
Imagination internal to the mind's eye piercing,
Morphing unduly to pressure eclipsed by inner turmoil,
Dancing a two-step, pirouette for an escape.
The shades a blur, colours all in disarray
Donning the veil of cunning intrigue.

Stay in the Game

Dare to dream.
Keep it real.
Up the stream,
Pedal to wheel,
Find your steam.
Made of steel,
Above the beam,
How so surreal.

Little Words

Who boasts and speaks in haste?
Is it not the one who hastily seeks gratification,
A pedestal for edification?
Is not a pit dug in full sight for travesty?
Once in, there is no way out.
Speak of limited words of meaning lifted high,
Eloquence of humility on the path well worn
Bearing bountiful fruit of seasons sure,
Ripe of actions pure and achievements that endure.
Fools be wise, keep it clear, shut the door.

From Another Planet

My wisdom is not of this world.
When I speak to the people
They do not understand.
Their hearts long for the things of this world.
I share of the things beyond and above
That imparts life on the person willing to accept.
I appear awkward in this world.
My actions do not conform to the way they want to do things.
In my oddness there is power, love, and self-discipline.
I receive my guidance and directions from the heavens,
The One who knows all things from beginning to end.
I do not rely on my knowledge
Since it is merely foolishness.
I trust in the One who has called me
To impart his truths to a world lost.
My obedience is to One truth, way, and life.
There is no other way for me.

The Tongue's Power

The tongue has power,
Fire-breathing dragon kind of power
To heal, to destroy, and be magical in nature,
Sending errant darts and gentle words.
Caution is a tale not revealed
Lest the fly on the wall carry it away
To distant lands and sources astray.
Exercise wisely with patience and scrutiny.
Benefits befall your destiny.
Clothed in purple linen and lined in fine gold,
So do the words adorn mind and soul.

Time's Up

Time comes; time goes.
It may be short; it may be long.
As it starts, so it must stop.
Eternal is our hearts
Searching greater accolades.
Finality is evident.
No one can predict
Serenity in the morning
Giving way to dread.
Fragility of each moment
Advancing one more step
Till the clock stand still.

Emptied

I am silenced.
I am not able to boast anymore.
I long for nothing more.
I am emptied of worldly pursuits.
I walk a narrow path.
I enter a small gate.
I am called to finish a task.
I know of no other way.

THIRD QUARTER

Uplift

Dew nourishes open fields.
Your beauty is your appeal.
Red roses bloom in an array of splendour.
Your heart pulses with its generous wonder.
Sun brightens the early dawn.
Your presence uplift and disarm.

Nothing Better

This is the day the Lord has made. Be glad and rejoice in it.

By the sweat of your brow, you will eat your food until you return to the ground, since from it you were taken; for dust you are and to dust you will return.

A person can do nothing better than to eat and drink and find satisfaction in their work.

There is nothing better for a person than to be joyful and do good while they live.

There is nothing better for a person than to enjoy their work, because that is their lot.

It is good and proper for a person to eat and drink, and to find satisfaction in their toilsome labour under the sun during the few days of life God has given them—for this is their lot.

It is commended to enjoy life, because nothing is better for a person under the sun than to eat and drink and be glad. Then joy will accompany them in their work all the days of life God has given them under the sun. Go, eat your food with gladness, and drink with a joyful heart, for it is now that God favours what you do. Always be clothed in white, and always anoint your head with oil. Enjoy life with your spouse, who you love, all the days of this meaningless life that God has given you under the sun—all your meaningless days. For this is your lot in life and in your toilsome labour under the sun.

Whatever your hand finds to do, do it with all your might, for in the grave, where you are going, there is neither working nor planning nor knowledge nor wisdom. Be joyous, young one, while you are young, and let your heart give you joy in the days of your youth. Follow the ways of your heart and whatever your eyes see but know that for all these things God will bring you to judgement. Therefore, fear God and keep his commandments, for this is the whole duty of humanity. God will bring every deed into judgement, including every hidden thing, whether it is good or evil.

Risk and Reward

Not everyone is willing to accept the same risks.

The risks we take are the risks that we expect to receive a reward.

The rewards we anticipate and hope for are envisioned based on the path we travel.

The time and effort we exert in the pursuit of the reward will have a correlated impact in the degree of success of the reward. Time and opportunity have a significant effect on attaining the rewards. To the extent that we chase after the rewards, according to the risks, we must also be prepared to accept the consequences as an alternative byproduct. There is no reward without a risk at hand. The risk at hand ushers in a myriad of consequences unseen. One must choose the price they are willing to pay to receive the reward from the risk at hand, understanding that the consequences may be grave.

The Best Bet

When we bet on the things of this world, the world takes away what we have anted up.

We expect a return for what we invest. We may receive an initial return on our bet but in the long view picture, the world robs what we have invested. Yet, when we store up our treasures in God's treasure chest, he ensures that the return will be so overflowing that we cannot contain it. It will be more than we put in and it will not be destroyed by anything. The reward from God is guaranteed, while the return from the world is deceptive and empty. Therefore, the best return is to bet on God rather than to bet on the world. Seek first his kingdom and righteousness and all your needs will be provided.

Skin Colour

What choice does my skin colour make?
Being born.
Being hungry.
Being sick.
Being loved.
Eventually dying.
What does skin colour have to do with anything
Except for appearance,
Made in the image of God.

obstacles

Up and down,
Round and round,
Over the mound
We go.

Through the tunnel,
Under the bridge,
Around the corner
We turn.

On the track,
Across the trail,
Hiking the hills
We race.

Jump the hoop,
Hurdle the fence,
Catapult the vault
We phrase.

All of them
Obstacles to navigate.

Aftermath

The surface is polished as dressed stone,
The outer edges draped in fine linen,
The extremities adorned with exquisite gems,
The speech refined of a master orator.
Yet something lurks in the regions unknown,
The deep, dark, distressed pit of the heart
Where scary, dangerous monsters struggle to escape
The cavernous confines of Sheol.
A moment of distraction as the pressures rise,
The beasts, beneath, ascend to thrive,
Revealing the truth of a hidden life
Poured out in action beyond belief,
Leaving a trail of debris in the aftermath.

Reverberation

What you see is not what it will be.
What you hear will be made clear.
Things of long ago are buried in remembrance.
Things to come shine clarity of days gone by.
Hopes for tomorrow echo hopes of today.
Tears, sorrows, and pains are our course for the day.
Will it always be this way?
When will it end?
How will it end?
On and on it goes.
Round and round, it comes around.
How will I know?
When will I know?
Heaven and Earth I know
Will be no more.
All will be new,
Cleansed and pure
From promises assured.
New Heaven and Earth,
A hope for sure.
No tears, sorrows, and pains of yore,
Rejoicing evermore.

Finishing What You Start

At the starting block I begin,
Unclear of the finish line.
A race to be run,
A host of challengers to chase,
Am I able, can I run, can I win, will I finish?
I am on a course prepared for me and me alone.
I see competition, but are they, my competitors?
Some are big; others are small.
Do I measure up at all?
I assess my chances and hopes of success.
Do I measure up or falter to my core?
I am unsure of this journey stirring in my soul.
I am exhilarated to even have the chance.
What are the risks?
What are the rewards?
I cannot see past the line.
It is too far away.
Can I cross it?
Can I win?
What are my chances?
Bang, the guns go.
Out the blocks I stroll,
Mustering my legs to follow.
A gallop, a glide along my flight.
Clickety Clack, Clickety Clack,
My feet and my heart.
I am only halfway down the track.
Some are ahead and some are behind.
Breathe, relax, and do not fret.
What fear is there to reach the end?

I strengthen my resolve.
I raise my head to glance.
A distance remains to go.
Scared and trembling, I know.
What do I have to show?
Maintaining my form which is the norm,
A style and technique my own.
Can I win?
Can I cross the line?
Time and chance speak aloud.
Give it your all.
Just finish what you start.

Sight

What are you pointing at?
I do not see what you are pointing at.
Why are you pointing?
Do you see something I do not see?
Do you know something I do not know?
I am confused.
You are confusing me.
I would like to see what you are pointing at.
How can I see if you do not tell me?
Open my eyes so that I can see what you are seeing.
I am in the dark.
You say there it is.
I do not see.
How can you see what I do not see?
Do you have a special vision that I do not have?
How can I access your vision unless I have your eyes?
You say my vision is what I see
From my knowledge, experience, and training.
You see what you see, and I see what I see.
For both to have the same vision
They must have sight—seeing the same thing together.

Only You, Lord

Only in you do I find strength.
Only in you do I find guidance.
Only in you do I find security.
Only in you do I find peace.
Only in you do I find love.
Only in you do I find life.
Only through you I am saved,
Jesus Christ.

Wish

Wish upon a star.
Ask whatever you wish.
Ask for it in prayer.
To bear much fruit each year,
Believe,
Receive,
Cup overflowing
With goodness and love
Showering.

Song of Praise

I waited patiently.
He lifted me out.
He set my feet.
He put forth a new song,
A hymn of praise.
"Here I am, I have come."
I desire to do your will.
I proclaim righteousness.
I do not seal my lips.
I do not hide.
I speak of you.
I do not conceal.

Love Given

Love cannot be bought.
Love is given.
Love is freedom,
A heart bestowed of truth.
Truth unselfishly given,
Unreserved and true.
Beyond depth, width, breadth,
Unfathomable.

Kids Away

What a lovely feeling!
Emptiness all around.
Calling out their names,
Bouncing off the wall.
Pictures show the faces.
Silence still abounds.
A longing for a hug,
A smile, a laugh, or a kiss.
There is a ring in the air.
The phone is always near.
Voices echo, "I miss you."
A resting of the soul,
But nothing changes this
One fact:
My kids are away!

FOURTH QUARTER

The Letter Opener and Pen Cover

I lost my letter opener a few months ago.
I searched all over the office and home and could not find it.
My daughter lost a pen cover a couple of days ago in the office.
I searched around the office and could not locate.
In both circumstances, I was bothered.
I really needed to use my letter opener to open all the mail.
I had to find another alternative that was convenient.
The pen cover was not as serious, but it was something
That I felt should not have happened, but it did.
I am very particular about finding things immediately when they are lost.
I was disturbed when I did not find them.
I realized that I could turn everything upside down to find these objects
But in their due time they will be revealed.
Well, this was the case.
While looking for the pen cover, I found the letter opener.
Just yesterday, I came across the pen cover when moving the computer keyboard.
The revelation of these findings dawned on me today.
All things are in our sight, but we must be patient to have them revealed in proper time.
We must wait for the barriers before our eyes to be removed.
When they are lifted, we will locate the things we are searching for.

Landing Somewhere

Shoot for something.
Land somewhere.
Shoot for the stars.
Land on the clouds.
Shoot for the moon.
Land on the stars.
Shoot for the sun.
Land on the moon.
Shoot for heaven.
Land in God's lap.

Nature's Curtain Call

Rustling leaves echo afar.
Water ripples, its waves shallow.
Billowy air tickling senses ajar,
Harmonies in cadence orchestrated,
Nature bows to one unseen.

Ode to the Fool

Beauty is fleeting,
Wealth deceptive.
Clothes masquerade the body.
Heart stores its secrets.
Tongue crumbles the soul.
Eyes scorch as the blazing sun.
Mind surveys the land.
Feet traverse the sacred places.
Hands capture treasured spoils.
Words are sweet,
Whispers enchanting,
Gifts disarming,
Favour demanding.
Look once, listen twice, and answer thrice,
Not to be fooled.

Freedom To Be Me

No eloquence in speech.
No trait to enamour.
Child full of energy,
Amazed by wonders unimaginable.
Stars glittering brightly,
Paths unbeknownst.
World coming and going,
New day becoming old.
Young succumbing to age,
Nothing of worth.
Arrays of thought encircling,
Choices to behold.
Emotions bubbling to explode,
Kaleidoscope of passions unheard.
Move forward, action taken,
Opportunity and chance unforsaken.
Door open, door close.
Time expire, dreams retire.
Remembrance only to inspire,
Freedom to be me.

I Care

I don't care what you wear
Or the colour of your hair.
It is because of you.

I don't care what you do
And why you do it.
It is because of you.

I don't care what you have
Or have not.
It is because of you.

I don't care if you talk a lot
Or a little.
It is because of you.

I don't care if you know something
Or everything.
It is because of you.

I don't care about the colour of your skin
Or if you're pretty in pink.
It is because of you.

I don't care about the language you speak
Or if you sign.
It is because of you.

I care!

War

Brother, Brother,
I want what you have.
Give me what you have.

Sister, Sister,
I want what you have.
Give me what you have.

Brother, Brother,
I don't like you.
I hate you.

Sister, Sister,
I don't like you.
I hate you.

Brother, Brother,
You make me sick.
I am coming for you.

Sister, Sister,
You make me sick.
I am going to get you.

My Anxiety

The sun scorches the landscape.
The moon elevates the tidal waves
Eroding the escarpment.
The volcano trembles at its core
Before its eruption.
The earth rattles and shakes,
Splitting a divide.
The cloudy skies cast their dark shadows.
Pouring rain ends my parade.
The monsoon washes away the hopes.
The winter freezes all extremities.
Mother Nature has not been kind.

Playful Song

The birds and the bees
Under the sycamore tree,
Lovely as these they sang to me.

Music so sweet,
Heavenly, and meek,
I could not but listen
To harmony complete.

A symphony of song
Echoed throughout,
Wonderful the sound
That searched me out.

Sum Zero

I entered with nothing,
No credits to my account,
No accolades to be found.
Alive on a distant island,
A chasm of time away,
Future stored in a foreign land,
My past on distant shores.
Stumble, fall, and dust myself off.
Continue the course,
Nice to be known.
Hustle, bustle, and put on a show.
Cheers euphoric smiles enticing,
Adrenalin intoxicating,
More, More, More!
Victory today,
Defeat in repeat.
Stay in the game.
Chances be sure
A mark to be made
Over and over again.
What do I gain?

On the Pond

Pond the lily pad.
Pond the stream.
Pond the river.
Pond the ocean.
Pond the sea,
Taking in the breeze.

Moments in Time

Minute by minute,
Hour by hour,
Building a strong tower.

Day by day,
Year by year,
Nothing to fear.

Frame by frame,
Picture by picture,
What do you capture?

Wall by wall,
Mirror by mirror,
It should be clearer.

A Whisper

Listen, Listen.
Do you hear my voice?
I call out to you.
Do you hear my voice?
A silent whisper in your ear,
Conversations of deepest care,
What should I do?
How should I respond?
Has my imagination gone beyond?
I hear the voice in my heart
Echoing a message.
Do I respond?
I must answer the call,
A charge of action
Of heart, soul, and mind.

Everything About You

Your beauty does not come from the clothes you wear
Or the comb in your hair.

Your beauty does not come from the gems around your neck
Or the amount on a cheque.

Your beauty does not come from the fragrance in the air
Or the smile you share.

Your beauty comes from the sugar, spice, and all things nice!

Do What You Say

Say what you say.
Say what you mean,
Polite and clean.

Do what you say.
Do what you do
So be it true.

Give what you say.
Give it today
And do not delay.

Live what you say,
Duplicity to slay
Life on display.

OVERTIME

Downside Up

If a mountain were downside up,
It would be a top.
If there were no traffic signs,
There would be no place to stop.
If the markets continue to drop,
There will be nowhere to shop.
If my teeth all fall out,
I could not chop.
If all the bubbles fizz,
There is no pop.
If the farmer fades away,
We have no crop.
This all happens when
Downside turns up.

What Do You Want From Me?

Looking back at me,
What do you see?
Tall, brown, and free,
I will not be deceived.

A lesson to learn,
Decisions to be discerned,
Possessions for the return,
The rest to burn.

Life, pure and faultless,
A picture to digest,
Avoiding all the tests,
Peace, patience, some rest.

History Connected

Chromosome X, Y, Z,
Carrying Ps and Qs,
One, two, a tree
From Adam and Eve.
My father, my mother,
The lines between,
Black, red, yellow, and white,
A rainbow that unites
Across land, over sea,
Reflections in me.

Intrusion

I have nowhere else to roam
Under the dome.
Where treacherous creatures
Are sown
A mysterious one
Was grown
That sat on a throne
And said
Everything postpone.
Now,
Work invades my home.

Skyscrapers

The poor look for cover to protect from the rain.
The rich build skyscrapers to measure their vain.
Children sit in the streets hoping for something to eat.
On fine dining tables there is plenty of meat.
Ghettos dig through the rubble for anything of worth.
High society leave their trail in the dirt.
Hope is the carrot dangled for the poor
Left hanging by the rich from their door.

Cellphone

What value is my cellphone?
I can make a call.
I can text a message.
I can google an answer.
I can store my thoughts.
I can stay connected.
But, most of all,
I can see how beautiful I look.

You Don't See Me as You Pass By

My body trembles as I dance with memories in my head.
My conversations are with persons unknown.
I scrape the filthy floors for a morsel to eat.
I am fragranced with scents of my own.
You kiss me with your cigarette-stained lips left behind.
You watch me not seeing any of these.

The Approach

It is you, Father, who approach us.
It is you who reveal yourself to us.
It is you who come near to us.
It is you who walk with us.
In our sinful state we are unable to approach you.
It is you who see your servant in distress.
It is you who come to the rescue.
It is you who lay the path for us
To enter your presence.

I Am Alone

I am alone walking
To school.
I am alone coming
Home.
I am alone playing
On the playground.
I am alone toiling
My trade.
I am alone working,
Making ends meet.
I am alone sleeping.
There are no other feet.
I am alone dreaming,
Tired in retreat.
I am alone living
In a crowded world.

Broken

Normal is as can be.
Why has all this happened to me?
Bent, broken, no relief,
Travel with wheels my legs,
Structures of stone my crutch.
Climbing a throne of stairs
To my pavement, a bed.
Misery, pain, my daily dose.
Sniff, puff, drinking them away.
Back, forth, a cycle to repeat.
How do I hold my dreams from defeat?
Look to my right, back to the left,
Out in front, broken as me.

A Shoe Left Alone

I wonder at all the miles you have travelled
To be abandoned and alone.
Your beginnings fresh and new,
Full of stories varied and true.
Many have walked in your shoe.
Now, lying on the sidewalk subdued,
Soul worn out from burdens untold,
Eyes of your laces drooping with unrest,
Tongue hanging limp in the morning mist,
Heel anchored at unlikely a place,
Soulmate lost some other space.
How lonely you look, no home to grace.

Representation

You're like night,
Full and bright,
Ever a light,
What a sight.
Have no fright.
Stand and fight
From your might.
Make it right.
What a delight.

Be Still and Know

I stand still in the blinding snow.
I climb the highest mountain to know.
I dive to the depths below
To open my mind aglow.
I plant a seed in soil
To reap from my toil.
Pressed and measured as oil,
Great gains from the spoils.
Spread it far and wide,
Cast it among the tides,
And just wait a while
Before you can smile.

Heart, Body, and Mind

The heart listens to the pulses of its desires.
The body follows what the heart craves.
The mind succumbs to the heart and body.
Keep heart, body, and mind sound and pure!

Jazz It Up

Bop Bippity Bop. Hop Hippity Hop. Doo Wop Ditty Wop. Shoo Wop Doo Wop.

Bee Wop Doo Wop. Hip Hop Shoo Wop. Hot Diggity. Hot Diggity. Hot Diggity Dog.

Shoo Wop Doo Wop. Scat Cat, Scat Cat, Shoo Wop Ditty Wop. Did Diddily Dee.

Did Diddly Doo. Shoo Wop Doo Dee. Doo Diddily Dee. Doo Wop Doo Dee.

Shoo Wop Dee Dee. Doo Diddily Dee. Doo Wop Doo Dee.

Smoke It, Joe. Smoke It, Joe. Just Let Them Know.

Doo Wee Lillily Lee. Shoo Wop Doo Diddily Dee.

Bee Bop Boo Bibbily Bee. Woo Wee Woo Wee. Shoo Wop Woo Wee.

Diddily Dee Lillily Lee. Shoo Wop Ooh Wee. Bo Diddily Dee. Shoo Wop Doo Dee.

Just Let it be. What do you see?

Doo Wop Doo Wee. Da Da Da Dee. Di Diddily Dee. Shoo Wop Bow Bee.

Da Dat Doo Dee. Shoo Willily Lee. Pa Pap Poo Diddily Dee. Da Da Dat Dee Dom Doo Dee. Shoo Wop Bow Bee. Pa Pa Pa Pee.

Ooh Woe Ooh Wee. Pa Pa Pa Pee. Bow Diddily Dee. Pa Pa Po Pee. Pa Pa Pa Pee.

Ooh Wee Ooh Wee. Doo Wop Ooh Wee. Shoo Pa Po Pee. Pa Pa Pa Pee.

Doo Diddily Lee. Shoo Wop Dee Diddily Dee. Pa Pa Pa Pee. Da Da Da Dee.

Shoo Wop Dee Dee. Pa Pa Pa Pee. Skiddily Diddily Dee. Wibbily Diddily Doo.

Doo Wop Doo Wop. Doo Wop Dee Dee. Da Diddily Dee. Da Diddily Doo.

Do Wop Bow Bee. Ba Bop Bow Bee. Doo Diddily Dee. Shoo Wop Bow Bee.

Bee Bop Bow Bee. Bow Diddily Dee. Shoo Womp Po Pee. Pa Pa Pa Pee.

Jazzamatazz. Razzamatazz. Scat Cat Scat Cat. Doo Dazz.

Post-Game Message

I am grateful to God for the ride he provided through the bad, good, and blessed moments of a presence on Earth.

In conclusion, this journey would not be meaningful for me to share if it were not made possible by Jesus Christ, my Lord and Saviour.

Through Christ, all that I have accomplished was made possible because of his guidance.

All that I am and all that I do is summed up in this poem to God. It is the cry of my heart to my Lord and Saviour for all the blessings showered upon my life.

Glory to God

Jesus is my God,
My King, My Lord, My Saviour,
My Refuge, My Provider, My Healer,
My Strength, My Shield, My Protector,
My Peace, My Patience, My Rest,
My Understanding, My Knowledge, My Wisdom,
My Way, My Life, My Love,
My One, My All, My Everything.

www.ingramcontent.com/pod-product-compliance
Lightning Source LLC
LaVergne TN
LVHW011850060526
838200LV00054B/4272